Angry

A CHERRYTREE BOOK

This edition first published in 2007
by Cherrytree Books, part of
The Evans Publishing Group Limited
2A Portman Mansions
Chiltern St
London
W1U 6NR

Printed in Malaysia

British Library Cataloguing in Publication Data

Amos, Janine
Angry. - 2nd ed. - (Feelings)
1. Anger - Juvenile literature
I. Title
155.4'1247

ISBN 978 184234477 4
First published in paperback1997

CREDITS
Editor: Louise John
Designer: D. R. ink
Production: Jenny Mulvanny

VISIT OUR WEBSITE
Evans
www.evansbooks.co.uk

Angry

By Janine Amos
Illustrated by Gwen Green

CHERRYTREE BOOKS

Ian's story

Ian fixed the last pieces of Lego together. It had taken him a long time to build – but it was the best model he'd ever made.

"Look at my space buggy!" said Ian. Very slowly he carried the model across to the table and put it down. Ian's brother Tim came to look.

"It's great!" said Tim. He turned one of the wheels round carefully. "Can I play with it – just while you're at football?"

Ian didn't really want anyone to touch his model.

"Let him. Don't be mean!" called Ian's mum from the front room.

"Promise you won't drop it?" said Ian. Tim promised.

Ian's team lost at football. When he got home he was tired. He threw down his sportsbag and went into the kitchen. Tim was there, playing with his friend Justin. They were playing with Lego.

Ian looked at the table. His space buggy had gone.

"Where's my model?" asked Ian. But the others were busy. They didn't hear him. Ian went across to Tim.

"Where's my space buggy?" Ian said again, in a loud voice.

"We wanted to make a windmill," said Tim.

"You've taken my model apart!" shouted Ian.

How do you think Ian is feeling now?

Ian kicked the Lego. It went right across the room and thumped against the wall. Then Ian punched Tim. Tim fell over and started to cry.

"I hate you!" shouted Ian.

Ian's mum heard the noise. She rushed into the room and shouted at the boys to stop fighting. But Ian didn't hear. Ian's mum pulled him away from Tim.

"Calm down," said Ian's mum.

"I won't!" Ian screamed. "He's ruined my model!"

"Upstairs – fast!" ordered Ian's mum.

Ian ran into his bedroom and slammed the door. He was shaking all over. He felt as if he would burst. Ian fell on to the bed. He started to cry with loud sobs. He was frightened.

Why do you think Ian is frightened?

Ian's mum came in and sat down next to him.

"Go away," Ian sobbed. "You're on Tim's side."

"I'm not," said his mum quietly.

At last Ian stopped shaking. He stopped crying too. But his throat hurt and he was very tired.

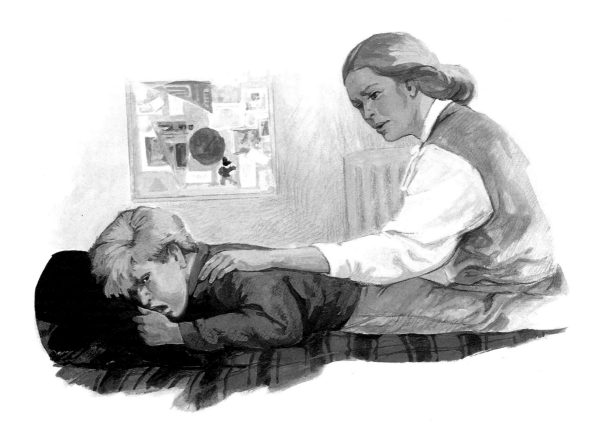

"Do you feel better now?" asked Ian's mum. Ian nodded.

"Your model was great, Ian," said his mum. "No wonder you were so angry."

"I nearly killed Tim," whispered Ian.

"No you didn't," said his mum. "You might have felt like it – but Tim's fine."

"I hate being angry," said Ian. "It's scary."

"Yes," said Ian's mum, "but there's nothing wrong with being cross. You shouldn't have hit Tim, though. You could have told him how cross you were. You could have asked him to help you make another model."

Later on, Ian built a new space buggy. When it was finished he put it down carefully on the table. Tim watched him.

"I'm sorry for breaking the other one," Tim said. "You were really mad, weren't you?"

"Yes," said Ian.

Tim looked again at the new model.

"This one's much better, though," he said.

How did Ian's mum help when Ian was feeling angry?

Feeling like Ian

Have you ever felt angry, like Ian? Have you ever felt so cross that you thought you might hurt someone else? If you have, you'll know how upsetting it can be. You may scream and shake. You may feel that anger has taken over your whole body. You feel out of control.

Good reasons

Often there's a good reason to be angry. Someone may break something which belongs to you. They may spoil something you've made. They may lose something of yours. You should let them know how angry you are. But getting out of control won't help things. And it may frighten you and make you feel bad afterwards.

Anger isn't bad

Anger isn't a bad feeling. Everyone gets cross sometimes. But there are many ways of showing anger. Sometimes, like Ian, your angry feelings may come out too strongly. Learning to show your feelings without getting too upset can be difficult. If you find it hard, ask for help. Tell an adult you trust.

Think about it

Read the stories in this book. Think about the people in the stories. Do you feel like them sometimes? Think what you've done when you've felt angry. Think what is the best thing for you to do next time you get cross.

Gina's story

It was sports day. The fifty metres race was about to begin. Gina waited at the starting line. She waved to her dad and her brother, Pip. Then she looked along the line at the other girls. Most of them seemed nervous. Only Anne was smiling. Anne was a good runner – but she wasn't as fast as Gina.

"Get ready!" called a voice. A whistle blew and the race started. Gina was the first away. She could feel the soft grass under her trainers. And she could hear the crowd cheering. Gina ran on and on. She knew that she could win.

Soon Gina could see the finishing line. On she went – and she knew that she was ahead of all the other girls. Then Gina tripped. She wobbled for a moment but she carried on running. She could feel her heart beating hard.

Then Anne raced past her to the finish. Gina couldn't believe it! It had all happened so quickly. People were crowding round.
"Well done, Anne. You were great! Bad luck, Gina," they said. But Gina turned away.

Gina's brother and her dad were waiting for her. She ran over to them.

"We can start the picnic now!" said Pip. But Gina wouldn't eat.

"You must be thirsty," said Gina's dad. He held out a carton of orange juice. Gina grabbed the carton amd threw it down on the grass. Then she stamped away.

How does Gina feel at this moment?
How do you think Gina's dad feels?

Gina watched her friends with their parents. Most of them were having picnics on the field. Everyone seemed to be having a great time. But Gina wasn't.

After a while Gina's dad came to sit next to her.

"Are you still feeling cross?" he asked. Gina nodded.

"Well, I think it's time to stop," said her dad. "You've missed the picnic and now you're spoiling the afternoon for yourself – and the rest of us."

"I can't help it," said Gina.

"You can try," said Gina's dad. He gave her a hug.

"I hate losing," said Gina.

"So do I," said her dad. "Losing is hard – and being a good loser is harder still."

Do you think Gina's dad is right?
Are you a good loser?

Feeling like Gina

Gina didn't win the race and it made her angry. She was cross with herself. If you are feeling like Gina, it helps to remember that everyone makes mistakes. You can't win all of the time. You can only do your best. Everyone has to learn how to be a good loser sometimes.

Let the anger go

If you're feeling like Gina, it may help to talk about it. Keeping your anger inside and thinking about how cross you are doesn't help. It didn't make Gina feel any better and she missed out on the picnic. So try to let the anger go. Take a deep breath and let it out slowly. Do it again and again.

Paul's story

Paul and his mum were at the railway station. They were going to stay with Auntie Kath. Paul had never been on a train before.

"We can have lunch on the train," said his mum. "And you can sit next to the window."

"Great!" said Paul. He was excited.

The station was very busy. Paul jumped as a train whizzed past.

"Keep close to me, Paul," said his mum. "Our train leaves from the next platform." Paul's mum picked up their suitcase and walked quickly down some steps. Paul ran along behind. Just then a crowd of people came towards him.

"Wait, Mum!" shouted Paul. All he could see were arms, legs and other people's cases. He couldn't see his mum anywhere.

Paul squeezed past all the other people. A big man gave him a push.

"I'm late," said the man, puffing.

"And I'm lost," thought Paul.

Paul got to the bottom of the steps and stood still. He wasn't sure what to do. He decided to wait for his mum.

Paul waited for a long time. He started to worry.
"I expect we've missed the train," he thought. "Or maybe Mum got on without me."

Then Paul heard someone calling his name. His mum came running towards him. But she didn't look happy.

"I told you to keep close to me!" she shouted. "Don't you dare get lost again!" Paul's eyes filled with tears. His face went red. Paul's mum took hold of his arm.

"Come on, we'll miss our train," she said.

Paul shook her away. "I'm not coming!" he shouted.

"Leave me alone!"

How do you think Paul's mum feels ?
How would you feel now if you were Paul ?

Paul was in a temper.

"It's your fault!" he screamed at his mum. "You went too fast!" Paul stamped his feet. He threw his new jacket on to the ground. "You lost me!" Paul was shaking. People in the station stopped to stare. Paul felt awful. He started to cry.

Just then there was an announcement.

"Listen," said Paul's mum. "It's our train!"

Paul's mum grabbed his arm and they both ran as fast as they could. Together they rushed up some more stairs. The train was ready to go. Paul and his mum were just in time.

By the time he sat down, Paul had stopped feeling cross. He was very tired.

"Shall we have some lunch?" asked Paul's mum. But Paul felt sick. He curled up in his seat.

"Come on," said his mum. "Let's make friends again."

"I'm sorry I shouted," said Paul's mum. "It wasn't your fault. I shouldn't have told you off."

"And I'm sorry," said Paul. "I was scared when I was lost."

"I was scared too," said his mum "That's why I shouted at you when I found you."

"I don't understand that," said Paul.

"And neither do I," said his mum laughing.

How did Paul and his mum make friends again

Do you find it easy to say you're sorry

Feeling like Paul

Paul's mum was scared and worried. That's why she shouted. But Paul didn't get lost on purpose. And when his mum shouted at him, he felt cross. He thought she was being unfair. So Paul got in a temper. He shouted and screamed. But getting in a temper didn't help Paul. It made him upset. It nearly made him miss the train.

Anger doesn't last

Tempers can feel as if they'll last for ever. And they can be scary. It helps to remember that very angry feelings never last. And you can always make friends again, no matter how cross you've been with someone.

Saying sorry

Arguing with friends and people you love can be upsetting. Saying sorry is a good way to end an argument. It shows that your angry outburst is over. It shows that you're ready to be friends again. And talking it over afterwards, as Paul and his mum did, will make you both feel better.

Think about it

Think about the stories in this book. Ian, Gina and Paul got angry for different reasons. Ian was angry because something he made was broken. Gina was angry with herself because she made a mistake. And Paul got in a temper because his mum shouted at him for something that wasn't his fault. They all showed their anger in different ways and they didn't feel any better until they'd let the anger go. Talking helped them. If you're feeling angry and upset, try talking it over with an adult you trust. Talking will help you too.

If you are feeling frightened or unhappy, don't keep it to yourself. Talk to an adult you can trust, like a parent or a teacher. If you feel really alone, you could telephone one of these offices. Remember, there is always someone who can help.

ChildLine
Freephone 0800 1111

The Line
ChildLine helpline for young people living away from home
Freephone 0800 884444
3.30pm to 9.30pm (weekdays)
2pm to 8pm (weekends)

NSPCC Child Protection Line
Phone 0808 800 5000

The Samaritans
Phone 08457 909090